I. INTRODUCTION

This report is the latest in a series on cigarette sales, advertising, and promotion that the Federal Trade Commission ("Commission") has prepared since 1967.

The statistical tables appended to this report provide information on domestic sales and advertising and promotional activity by the largest U.S. cigarette manufacturers. The tables were compiled from data contained in special reports submitted to the Commission pursuant to compulsory process by: Altria Group, Inc.; Commonwealth Brands, Inc.; Lorillard, Inc.; Reynolds American, Inc.; and Vector Group Ltd.[1]

II. TOTAL SALES AND ADVERTISING AND PROMOTIONAL EXPENDITURES

The total number of cigarettes reported sold by the major manufacturers decreased by 11.0 billion units (4.1 percent) from 2012 to 2013. Advertising and promotional expenditures decreased during that same period, falling from $9.168 billion to $8.948 billion. The largest single category of these expenditures in 2013 was price discounts paid to cigarette retailers or wholesalers in order to reduce the price of cigarettes to consumers, which accounted for $7.642 billion (85.4 percent of total advertising and promotional expenditures).[2]

III. CIGARETTES SOLD AND GIVEN AWAY

Tables 1, 1A, and 1B display annual cigarette sales by the manufacturers to wholesalers and retailers. Table 1B displays the total number of cigarettes sold in the years 2011 through 2013. In 2013, the five major domestic cigarette manufacturers sold 256.7 billion cigarettes

---

[1] Although the number and identity of the companies reporting cigarette data has varied over the more than 45 years that the Commission has issued these reports, these five companies have been the recipients of the Commission's compulsory process orders since 2008.

[2] The advertising and promotion expenditure figures contained in this report are in nominal dollars and have not been adjusted for inflation.

domestically, down from 267.7 billion in 2012. The Commission is not reporting the number of cigarettes given away[3] in 2013, because – as in 2011 and 2012 – only one company reported such giveaways.[4]

IV. ADVERTISING AND PROMOTIONAL EXPENDITURES BY CATEGORY

Tables 2 through 2E show the amounts spent on cigarette advertising and promotion for the years 1970, and 1975 through 2013.[5] These tables list the amounts spent on the different types of media advertising (*e.g.*, magazines) and sales promotion activities (*e.g.*, distribution of cigarette samples), and also give the percentage of the total amount spent for the various types of advertising and promotion.

Table 2E shows that overall, the major manufacturers spent $8.948 billion on cigarette advertising and promotion in 2013, a decrease from the $9.168 billion spent in 2012.[6]

The companies reported spending $50.6 million on magazine advertising in 2013, an

---

[3] Cigarettes given away include all cigarettes distributed for free, whether through sampling, coupons for free product, "buy 3 packs, get 1 free" type offers, or otherwise, as long as those cigarettes were not reported as sold. For years prior to 2001, the Commission required the manufacturers to report the number of cigarettes they sold but not the number they gave away. It is possible that in those earlier years, some manufacturers included in their sales figures some cigarettes that were actually given away.

[4] Because only one company reported giveaways the Commission does not report the number of cigarettes given away in order to avoid potential disclosure of individual company data.

[5] The reported figures include all advertising and promotional expenditures related to cigarettes, regardless of whether such expenditures would constitute "commercial speech" or would be protected from law enforcement action under the First Amendment.

[6] Definitions of the advertising and promotional expenditure categories appear in the Appendix to this report. If only one company reported spending money on a particular type of advertising or promotion, that category appears as "N/A" on Tables 2D and 2E and the expenditures are included in the "All Others" category, to avoid potential disclosure of individual company data. For this reason, the Commission is not separately reporting the amounts spent in 2013 on newspapers, sampling, telephone advertising, or Internet advertising, other than on a company's own web site.

increase from the $27.9 million they spent in 2012. The Commission is not reporting the amount spent on newspaper advertising.

Spending on "outdoor" advertising increased slightly from $2.2 million in 2012 to $2.3 million in 2013. Since 2002, "outdoor" advertising has been defined to mean billboards; signs and placards in arenas, stadiums, and shopping malls (whether they are open air or enclosed); and any other advertisements placed outdoors, regardless of their size, including those on cigarette retailer property. Before 2002, "outdoor" advertising was not precisely defined and it was not clear that signs in arenas, stadiums, shopping malls, or on retailer property would have been reported in this category.

As they have since 2001, the companies reported no expenditures on transit advertising (*i.e.*, advertising in or on private or public vehicles or any transportation facility) in 2013.

Spending on point-of-sale materials (ads posted at the retail location but excluding outdoor ads on retailer property) declined from $67.9 million in 2012 to $55.7 million in 2013.

Since 2002, the "promotional allowance" category has been replaced by four separate categories: price discounts, promotional allowances paid to retailers, promotional allowances paid to wholesalers, and other promotional allowances. As noted above, the largest of these categories was price discounts paid to cigarette retailers or wholesalers in order to reduce the price of cigarettes to consumers (*e.g.*, off-invoice discounts, buy downs, and voluntary price reductions), which accounted for expenditures of $7.642 billion in 2013 (down from $7.802 billion in 2012). In addition, the industry spent $291.3 million in 2013 (down from $335.1 million in 2012) on promotional allowances paid to cigarette retailers in order to facilitate the sale or placement of cigarettes (*e.g.*, payments for stocking, shelving, displaying, and merchandising brands, volume rebates, and incentive payments); $397.2 million (up from $391.1 million) on promotional allowances paid to cigarette wholesalers (*e.g.*, payments for volume rebates, incentive payments, value-added services, and promotional executions); and $548,000 on promotional allowances paid to persons other than retailers and wholesalers.[7] When these four promotional allowance categories are combined, they total $8.332 billion, and account for 93.1 percent of all 2013 spending.

The Commission is not separately reporting the amount spent in 2013 giving cigarette samples to the public ("sampling distribution") because only one company reported spending in that category. "Sampling" includes the distribution of cigarettes for consumer testing or evaluation outside the company's facility, and the distribution of coupons for free cigarettes when no purchase or payment is required to obtain the coupons or cigarettes.

In 2013, $3.0 million was spent on branded specialty item distribution through the mail, at promotional events, or by any means other than at the point-of-sale with the purchase of cigarettes; $29.5 million was spent distributing non-branded, non-cigarette items in connection with the marketing or promotion of cigarettes.[8] In 2012, those figures had been $1.7 million and $26.1 million, respectively.

Expenditures for the adult-only public entertainment category declined from $113.6 million in 2012 to $104.6 million in 2013. This category includes public entertainment events that take place in an adult-only facility (*e.g.*, sponsorship of bar nights or concerts) and display the name or logo of a company's cigarettes or otherwise refer to cigarettes. The companies reported no 2013 expenditures on public entertainment events in non-adult-only facilities that display the name or

---

[7] The Commission is not separately reporting the amount spent in 2012 on promotional allowances paid to persons other than retailers and wholesalers because only one company reported spending in that category.

[8] Specialty item distribution includes the practice of selling or giving to consumers non-cigarette items, such as T-shirts, caps, sunglasses, key chains, lighters, and sporting goods.

logo of a company's cigarettes or otherwise refer or relate to cigarettes.

All reporting companies stated that in 2013 they spent no money on sponsorships, endorsements and testimonials, or on audio-visual advertising. For 2012, they reported no spending on sponsorships and the Commission did not separately report the amounts spent on endorsements and testimonials or audio-visual advertising.

The companies reported spending $38.3 million for direct mail advertising in 2013, down from $45.6 million in 2012.[9]

The industry reported spending $248.8 million on coupons to reduce the retail cost of cigarettes in 2013 (an increase from the $239.6 million reported in 2012).[10]

Retail-value-added expenditures are the costs associated with offers such as "buy one, get one free" and "buy three, get a free T-shirt," where the bonus item is distributed at retail when the cigarettes are purchased. As they had in 2012, the companies reported spending no money on either category of retail-value-added in 2013.

In 2013, the companies reported spending $15.4 million on advertising on company websites, down from the $21.4 million they reported in 2012. The Commission is not separately reporting the amount spent in 2013 on Internet advertising other than company websites because only one company reported spending in that category.

The companies reported no spending in 2013 on "social media marketing on Web sites or other online services or communities, including but not limited to social networking sites, microblogging sites, content-sharing sites, and blogs," just as they have each year since the

---

[9] This category does not include direct mail containing coupons, which is reported in the coupons category.

[10] As noted above, when coupons are distributed for free cigarettes and no purchase is required to redeem them, such activities are reported as "sampling," not as "coupons."

Commission started requesting these data.

The Commission requires the cigarette manufacturers to report the amounts they spent advertising and promoting sports and sporting events.[11] This question is separate from, and duplicative of, the reporting of the individual various advertising and promotion categories. For example, money spent on a magazine advertisement promoting a cigarette-branded sports tournament open to those of all ages would be reported under the category "general-audience public entertainment" and would also be reported as an expenditure on "sports and sporting events." As they have each year since 2010, the companies reported that they did not spend any money on sports and sporting events in 2013.

Since 2001, the Commission has required the manufacturers to report expenditures on advertisements directed to youth or their parents that are intended to reduce youth smoking. The companies reported spending $1.9 million in 2013.[12] Over the previous seven years, they had reported expenditures of $57.7 million (2006), $20.7 million (2007), $11.5 million (2008), $8.1 million (2009), and $4.4 million (2010), $2.9 million (2011), and $2.2 million (2012). These figures do not include contributions to third parties that engage in such programs.

Cigarette manufacturers reported that neither they nor anyone working for them or on their behalf paid money or any other form of compensation in connection with the production or filming of any motion picture or television show in 2013, or paid money or any other form of compensation

---

[11] This includes expenditures for: (1) the sponsoring, advertising, or promotion of sports or sporting events; support of an individual, group, or sports team; and purchase of or support for equipment, uniforms, sports facilities, and/or training facilities; (2) all expenditures for advertising in the name of the cigarette company or any of its brands in a sports facility, on a scoreboard, or in conjunction with the reporting of sports results; and (3) all expenditures for functional promotional items (clothing, hats, etc.) connected with a sporting event.

[12] These expenditures are not included in the $8.948 billion reported in Table 2E (cigarette expenditures by category for 2013).

to anyone engaged in product placement in motion pictures or television shows. The companies also reported that neither they nor anyone working for them or on their behalf: (1) sought, solicited, granted approval, or otherwise gave permission for the appearance of any cigarette product or cigarette brand imagery in any motion picture, television show, or video appearing on the Internet, or (2) engaged in social media marketing that promoted any cigarette brand or variety or used cigarette brand imagery. One company did report having video advertising on a website restricted to age-verified smokers 21 or older and allowing the posting of user-generated content on that restricted website.

The expenditure data reported in Tables 2 through 2E were not collected in their present form until 1975. Therefore, Table 3 reports advertising expenditures from 1963 through 1974.

V.   TAR RATINGS, FILTERS, LENGTH, AND FLAVOR

Tables 4 and 4A give the domestic market share of cigarettes with tar ratings of 15 mg or less for the years 1967 through 2013. The data for the years since 1982 are further broken down into sub-categories according to tar ratings, *e.g.*, 3 mg or less, 6 mg or less, etc. (categories are presented cumulatively).

The tar yield data reported to the Commission appear to show decreases from 2012 to 2013 in the market share of cigarettes with tar yields of 3 mg or less, 6 mg or less, 9 mg or less, 12 mg or less, and 15 mg or less. The Commission notes, however, that its compulsory process orders requesting data for 2011 through 2013 have required the companies only to report tar, nicotine, and carbon monoxide data that they have available; they were not required to conduct additional testing. Consequently, market share comparisons within these years or to previous years may no longer be possible.

As shown in Tables 5 and 5A, filtered cigarettes have dominated the market since the

Commission began collecting this information in 1963. Filtered cigarettes account for 99.7 percent of the market in 2013.

Table 6 provides the market share of the various cigarette length categories. The King size (79-88 mm) category continues to be the biggest seller, with 57 percent of the market in 2013. This category is followed by the Long (94-101 mm) group, with 39 percent of the market.

Tables 7 and 7A give the market share of menthol and non-menthol cigarettes. In 2013, menthol cigarettes were 31 percent of the market, while non-menthols were 69 percent.

Table 8 shows the percentage of cigarettes that disclosed both tar and nicotine yields on their packs during the years 1994 through 2001; Table 8A shows the percentage that disclosed tar yields from 2002 to 2011. In 2013, as in every year since 2008, 0.0% of the overall cigarette market disclosed tar yields on the pack. Therefore, as the Commission first noted in its Cigarette Report for 2011, Table 8A will not be updated unless and until the companies resume printing tar yields on their product packaging.

TABLE 1

TOTAL DOMESTIC CIGARETTE UNIT SALES (IN BILLIONS OF INDIVIDUAL CIGARETTES)

YEAR	TOTAL SALES REPORTED BY CIGARETTE MANUFACTURERS*	UNIT CHANGE FROM PRIOR YEAR	% CHANGE FROM PRIOR YEAR	USDA CIGARETTE CONSUMPTION ESTIMATES
1963	516.5	–	–	523.9
1964	505.0	(11.5)	(2.2)	511.2
1965	521.1	16.1	3.2	528.7
1966	529.9	8.8	1.7	541.2
1967	525.8	5.9	1.1	549.2
1968	540.3	4.5	.8	545.7
1969	527.9	(12.4)	(2.3)	528.9
1970	534.2	6.3	1.1	536.4
1971	547.2	13.0	2.4	555.1
1972	561.7	14.5	2.7	566.8
1973	584.7	23.0	4.1	589.7
1974	594.5	9.8	1.7	599.0
1975	603.2	8.7	1.5	607.2
1976	609.9	6.7	1.1	613.5
1977	612.6	2.7	.4	617.0
1978	615.3	2.7	.4	616.0
1979	621.8	6.5	1.1	621.5
1980	628.2	6.4	1.0	631.5
1981	636.5	8.3	1.3	640.0
1982	632.5	(4.0)	(.6)	634.0
1983	603.6	(28.9)	(4.6)	600.0
1984	608.4	4.8	.8	600.4
1985	599.3	(9.1)	(1.5)	594.0
1986	586.4	(12.9)	(2.2)	583.8
1987	575.4	(11.0)	(1.9)	575.0
1988	560.7	(14.7)	(2.6)	562.5
1989	525.6	(35.1)	(6.3)	540.0
1990	523.7	(1.9)	(.4)	525.0
1991	510.9	(12.8)	(2.4)	510.0
1992	506.4	(4.5)	(.9)	500.0
1993	461.4	(45.0)	(8.9)	485.0
1994	490.2	28.8	6.2	486.0
1995	482.3	(7.9)	(1.6)	487.0
1996	484.1	1.8	0.4	487.0
1997	478.6	(5.5)	(1.1)	480.0
1998	458.6	(20.1)	(4.2)	465.0
1999	411.3	(47.2)	(10.3)	435.0
2000	413.9	2.6	.6	430.0

*   Cigarettes sold by manufacturers to wholesalers and retailers within the U.S. and to armed forces personnel stationed outside the U.S.

TABLE 1A

TOTAL DOMESTIC CIGARETTE UNITS SOLD AND GIVEN AWAY (2001-2010)
(IN BILLIONS OF INDIVIDUAL CIGARETTES)

YEAR	UNITS SOLD*	UNITS GIVEN AWAY**	TOTAL NUMBER SOLD AND GIVEN AWAY AS REPORTED BY MANUFACTURERS	UNIT CHANGE IN SOLD AND GIVEN AWAY FROM PRIOR YEAR†	PERCENT CHANGE IN SOLD AND GIVEN AWAY FROM PRIOR YEAR†	USDA CIGARETTE CONSUMPTION ESTIMATES
2001	398.3	3.9	402.2	–	–	425.0
2002	376.4	11.1	387.4	(14.8)	(3.7)	415.0
2003	360.5	7.1	367.6	(19.8)	(5.1)	400.0
2004	361.3	2.1	363.4	(4.2)	(1.1)	388.0
2005	351.6	3.0	354.6	(8.8)	(2.4)	376.0
2006	343.3	7.2	350.5	(4.1)	(1.2)	371.0
2007	337.7	5.0	342.8	(7.7)	(2.2)	***
2008	320.0	2.7	322.6	(20.2)	(5.9)	***
2009	290.6	0.1	290.7	(31.9)	(9.9)	***
2010	282	0.05	282.1	(8.7)	(3.0)	***

*   Cigarettes sold by manufacturers to wholesalers and retailers within the U.S. and to armed forces personnel stationed outside the U.S.

**   Cigarettes given away within the U.S. and to armed forces personnel stationed outside the U.S. Prior to 2001, the Commission did not ask about cigarettes given away, although some cigarettes given away may have been reported as sold.

***   USDA ceased reporting this data.

†   Because of rounding, changes from prior year's figures might only be approximate.

TABLE 1B

TOTAL DOMESTIC CIGARETTE UNITS SOLD (2011-2013)
(IN BILLIONS OF INDIVIDUAL CIGARETTES)

YEAR	UNITS SOLD*	UNITS CHANGE FROM PRIOR YEAR	PERCENT CHANGE FROM PRIOR YEAR†
2011	273.6	(8.6)	(3.0)
2012	267.7	(5.9)	(2.2)
2013	256.7	(11.0)	(4.1)

*   Cigarettes sold by manufacturers to wholesalers and retailers within the U.S. and to armed forces personnel stationed outside the U.S.

†   Because of rounding, changes from prior year's figures might only be approximate.

TABLE 2

DOMESTIC CIGARETTE ADVERTISING AND PROMOTIONAL EXPENDITURES FOR YEARS 1970, 1975-1985 (DOLLARS IN THOUSANDS)*

	1970	1975	1976	1977	1978	1979	1980	1981	1982	1983	1984	1985
Newspapers	$14,026 3.9%	$104,460 21.3%	$155,808 24.4%	$190,677 24.5%	$186,947 21.4%	$240,978 22.2%	$304,380 24.5%	$358,096 23.1%	$282,897 15.8%	$200,563 10.6%	$193,519 9.2%	$203,527 8.2%
Magazines	$50,018 13.9%	$131,199 26.6%	$148,032 23.2%	$173,296 22.2%	$184,236 21.1%	$257,715 23.8%	$266,208 21.4%	$291,227 18.8%	$349,229 19.5%	$388,365 20.4%	$425,912 20.3%	$395,129 16.0%
Outdoor	$7,338 2.0%	$84,329 17.2%	$102,689 16.1%	$120,338 15.4%	$149,010 17.0%	$162,966 15.0%	$193,333 15.6%	$228,081 14.7%	$266,925 14.9%	$295,226 15.5%	$284,927 13.6%	$300,233 12.1%
Transit	$5,354 1.5%	$10,852 2.2%	$19,341 3.0%	$21,530 2.8%	$22,899 2.6%	$21,151 2.1%	$26,160 2.0%	$21,931 1.4%	$24,135 1.3%	$26,652 1.4%	$25,817 1.2%	$33,136 1.3%
Point-of-Sale	$11,663 3.2%	$35,317 7.2%	$44,176 6.9%	$46,220 5.9%	$57,384 6.6%	$66,096 6.1%	$79,799 6.4%	$98,968 6.4%	$116,954 6.5%	$170,059 8.9%	$167,279 8.0%	$142,921 5.8%
Promotional Allowances	$33,789 9.4%	$72,018 14.7%	$82,523 12.9%	$108,227 13.9%	$125,148 14.3%	$137,111 12.7%	$179,094 14.4%	$229,077 14.8%	$272,269 15.2%	$366,153 19.3%	$363,247 17.3%	$548,877 22.2%
Sampling Distribution	$11,775 3.3%	$24,196 4.9%	$40,390 6.3%	$47,683 6.1%	$47,376 5.4%	$64,286 5.9%	$50,459 4.1%	$81,522 5.3%	$141,178 7.9%	$125,968 6.6%	$148,031 7.1%	$140,565 5.7%
Specialty Item Distribution	$5,652 2.6%	$10,088 2.1%	$20,030 3.1%	$35,797 4.6%	$48,281 5.5%	$62,029 5.7%	$69,248 5.6%	$115,107 7.5%	$95,246 5.3%	$127,186 6.6%	$140,431 6.7%	$211,429 8.5%
Public Entertainment	$544 0.2%	$8,484 1.7%	$7,946 1.3%	$9,538 1.2%	$11,590 1.3%	$10,783 1.0%	$16,914 1.4%	$37,423 2.4%	$63,168 3.5%	$76,648 4.0%	$59,988 2.9%	$57,581 2.3%
Other**	$220,841 61.1%	$10,311 2.0%	$18,182 2.8%	$26,157 3.4%	$42,100 4.8%	$60,310 5.6%	$56,694 4.6%	$86,226 5.6%	$181,813 10.1%	$123,951 6.5%	$286,035 13.7%	$443,043 17.9%
Total	$361,000 100%	$491,254 100%	$639,117 100%	$779,463 100%	$874,971 100%	$1,083,425 100%	$1,242,289 100%	$1,547,658 100%	$1,793,814 100%	$1,900,771 100%	$2,095,231 100%	$2,476,441 100%

* Because of rounding, sums of percentages may not equal 100 percent.

** Includes TV and Radio advertising expenditures of $207,324,000 and $12,492,000, respectively, for 1970. Broadcast advertising was banned after January 1, 1971. Expenditures for direct mail, endorsements, testimonials, and audio-visual are included in the "All Others" category to avoid potential disclosure of individual company data.

TABLE 2A

DOMESTIC CIGARETTE ADVERTISING AND PROMOTIONAL EXPENDITURES FOR YEARS 1986-1995 (DOLLARS IN THOUSANDS)*

	1986	1987	1988	1989	1990	1991	1992	1993	1994	1995
Newspapers	$119,629 5.0%	$95,810 3.7%	$105,783 3.2%	$76,993 2.1%	$71,174 1.8%	$48,212 1.0%	$35,467 0.7%	$36,220 0.6%	$24,143 0.5%	$19,122 0.4%
Magazines	$340,160 14.3%	$317,748 12.3%	$355,055 10.8%	$380,393 10.5%	$328,143 8.2%	$278,110 6.0%	$237,061 4.5%	$235,253 3.9%	$251,644 5.2%	$248,848 5.1%
Outdoor	$301,822 12.7%	$269,778 10.5%	$319,293 9.7%	$358,583 9.9%	$375,627 9.4%	$386,165 8.3%	$295,657 5.7%	$231,481 3.8%	$240,024 5.0%	$273,664 5.6%
Transit	$34,725 1.5%	$35,822 1.4%	$44,379 1.4%	$52,294 1.4%	$60,249 1.5%	$60,163 1.3%	$53,293 1.0%	$39,117 0.6%	$29,323 0.6%	$22,543 0.5%
Point-of-Sale	$135,541 5.7%	$153,494 5.9%	$222,289 6.8%	$241,809 6.7%	$303,855 7.6%	$344,580 7.4%	$366,036 7.0%	$400,943 6.6%	$342,650 7.1%	$259,035 5.3%
Promotional Allowances	$630,036 26.4%	$702,430 27.2%	$879,703 26.9%	$999,843 27.6%	$1,021,427 25.6%	$1,156,280 24.9%	$1,514,026 28.9%	$1,557,635 25.8%	$1,678,917 34.7%	$1,865,657 38.1%
Sampling Distribution	$98,866 4.1%	$55,020 2.1%	$74,511 2.3%	$57,771 1.6%	$100,893 2.5%	$56,970 1.2%	$49,315 0.9%	$40,202 0.7%	$6,974 0.1%	$13,836 0.3%
Specialty Item Distribution	$210,128 8.8%	$391,351 15.2%	$190,003 5.8%	$262,432 7.3%	$307,037 7.7%	$184,348 4.0%	$339,997 6.5%	$755,780 12.5%	$850,810 17.6%	$665,173 13.6%
Public Entertainment	$71,439 3.0%	$71,389 2.8%	$88,072 2.7%	$92,120 2.5%	$125,094 3.1%	$118,622 2.6%	$89,739 1.7%	$84,276 1.4%	$81,292 1.7%	$110,669 2.3%
Direct Mail	$187,057 7.9%	$187,931 7.3%	$42,545 1.3%	$45,498 1.3%	$51,875 1.3%	$65,002 1.4%	$34,345 0.7%	$31,463 0.5%	$31,187 0.7%	$34,618 0.7%
Endorsements & Testimonials	$384 0.0%	$376 0.0%	$781 0.0%	$0 0.0%	$0 0.0%	$0 0.0%	$0 0.0%	$0 0.0%	$0 0.0%	$0 0.0%
Coupons & Retail-Value-Added	**	**	$874,127 26.7%	$959,965 26.5%	$1,183,798 29.6%	$1,882,905 40.4%	$2,175,373 41.6%	$2,559,387 42.4%	$1,248,896 25.8%	$1,348,378 27.5%
Other***	$252,570 10.0%	$299,355 11.6%	$78,366 2.4%	$89,290 2.5%	$62,917 1.6%	$68,758 1.5%	$41,608 0.8%	$63,680 1.2%	$47,672 1.0%	$33,680 0.7%
Total	$2,382,357 100%	$2,580,504 100%	$3,274,853 100%	$3,616,993 100%	$3,992,008 100%	$4,650,114 100%	$5,231,917 100%	$6,035,437 100%	$4,833,532 100%	$4,895,223 100%

* Because of rounding, sums of percentages may not equal 100 percent.

** Prior to 1987, the Commission did not specifically collect information on Coupons & Retail-Value-Added.

*** Expenditures for audio-visual are included in the "All Others" category to avoid potential disclosure of individual company data.

DOMESTIC CIGARETTE ADVERTISING AND PROMOTIONAL EXPENDITURES
FOR YEARS 1996-2001 (DOLLARS IN THOUSANDS)*

	1996	1997	1998	1999	2000	2001
Newspapers	$14,067	$16,980	$29,444	$50,952	$51,652	$31,676
	0.3%	0.3%	0.4%	0.6%	0.5%	0.3%
Magazines	$243,046	$236,950	$281,296	$377,364	$294,916	$172,853
	4.8%	4.2%	4.2%	4.6%	3.1%	1.5%
Outdoor	$292,261	$295,334	$294,721	$53,787	$9,262	$8,241
	5.7%	5.2%	4.4%	0.7%	0.1%	0.1%
Transit	$28,865	$26,407	$40,158	$5,573	$4	$0
	0.6%	0.5%	0.6%	0.1%	0.0%	0.0%
Point-of-Sale	$252,619	$305,360	$290,739	$329,429	$347,038	$284,319
	4.9%	5.4%	4.3%	4.0%	3.6%	2.5%
Promotional Allowances	$2,150,838	$2,438,468	$2,878,919	$3,542,950	$3,913,997	$4,452,709
	42.1%	43.1%	42.8%	43.0%	40.8%	39.7%
Sampling Distribution	$15,945	$22,065	$14,436	$33,711	$22,330	$17,175
	0.3%	0.4%	0.2%	0.4%	0.2%	0.2%
Specialty Item Distribution	$544,345	$512,602	$355,835	$335,680	$327,826	$333,394
	10.7%	9.6%	5.3%	4.1%	3.4%	3.0%
Public Entertainment	$171,177	$195,203	$248,536	$267,379	$309,610	$312,366
	3.4%	3.4%	3.7%	3.3%	3.2%	2.8%
Direct Mail	$38,703	$37,310	$57,772	$94,610	$92,902	$133,947
	0.8%	0.7%	0.9%	1.2%	1.0%	1.2%
Endorsements & Testimonials	$0	$0	$0	$0	$0	$0
	0.0%	0.0%	0.0%	0.0%	0.0%	0.0%
Coupons		$552,550	$624,199	$531,004	$705,299	$602,110
	$1,308,708**	9.8%	9.3%	6.5%	7.4%	5.4%
Retail-Value-Added	25.6%	$970,363	$1,555,391	$2,559,883	$3,453,446	$4,761,792
		17.1%	23.1%	31.1%	36.0%	42.5%
Internet	$432	$215	$125	$651	$949	$841
	0.0%	0.0%	0.0%	0.0%	0.0%	0.0%
Other***	$46,696	$50,207	$61,584	$54,658	$63,395	$104,797
	0.9%	1.0%	0.9%	0.7%	0.7%	0.9%
Total	$5,107,700	$5,660,014	$6,733,157	$8,237,631	$9,592,627	$11,216,220
	100%	100%	100%	100%	100%	100%

* Because of rounding, sums of percentages may not equal 100 percent.
** Prior to 1997, Coupons and Retail-Value-Added were reported as a single category.
*** Expenditures for audio-visual are included in the "All Others" category to avoid potential disclosure of individual company data.

TABLE 2C
DOMESTIC CIGARETTE ADVERTISING AND PROMOTIONAL EXPENDITURES FOR YEARS 2002-2005
(DOLLARS IN THOUSANDS)*

	2002	2003	2004	2005
Newspapers	$25,538	$8,251	$4,913	$1,589
	0.2%	0.1%	0.0%	0.0%
Magazines	$106,852	$156,394	$95,700	$44,777
	0.9%	1.0%	0.7%	0.3%
Outdoor	$24,192	$32,599	$17,135	$9,821
	0.2%	0.2%	0.1%	0.0%
Transit	$0	$0	$0	$0
	0.0%	0.0%	0.0%	0.0%
Point-of-Sale	$260,902	$165,573	$163,621	$182,193
	2.1%	1.1%	1.2%	1.4%
Price Discounts	$7,873,835	$10,808,239	$10,932,199	$9,776,069
	63.2%	71.4%	77.3%	74.6%
Promotional Allowances – Retailers	$1,333,097	$1,229,327	$542,213	$435,830
	10.7%	8.1%	3.8%	3.3%
Promotional Allowances – Wholesalers	$446,327	$683,067	$387,758	$410,363
	3.6%	4.5%	2.7%	3.1%
Promotional Allowances – Other	$2,767	$2,786	$1,323	$1,493
	0.0%	0.0%	0.0%	0.0%
Sampling Distribution	$28,777	$17,853	$11,649	$17,211
	0.2%	0.1%	0.0%	0.1%
Specialty Item Distribution – Branded	$49,423	$9,195	$8,011	$5,255
	0.4%	0.1%	0.0%	0.0%
Specialty Item Distribution - Non-Branded	$174,201	$254,956	$216,577	$225,279
	1.4%	1.7%	1.5%	1.7%
Public Entertainment – Adult-Only	$219,016	$150,889	$140,137	$214,075
	1.8%	1.0%	1.0%	1.6%
Public Entertainment – General-Audience	$34,089	$32,849	$115	$152
	0.3%	0.2%	0.0%	0.0%
Sponsorships	$54,247	$31,371	$28,231	$30,575
	0.4%	0.2%	0.2%	0.2%
Endorsements & Testimonials	$0	$0	$0	$0
	0.0%	0.0%	0.0%	0.0%
Direct Mail	$111,319	$92,978	$93,836	$51,844
	0.9%	0.6%	0.7%	0.0%
Coupons	$522,246	$650,653	$751,761	$870,137
	4.2%	4.3%	5.3%	6.6%
Retail-Value-Added – Bonus Cigarettes	$1,060,304	$677,308	$636,221	$725,010
	8.5%	4.5%	4.5%	5.5%
Retail-Value-Added – Non-Cigarette Bonus	$24,727	$20,535	$14,343	$7,526
	0.2%	0.1%	0.1%	0.0%
Company Website	$940	$2,851	$1,401	$2,675
	0.0%	0.0%	0.0%	0.0%
Internet – Other	$0	$0	$0	$0
	0.0%	0.0%	0.0%	0.0%
Telephone	$679	$760	$346	$59
	0.0%	0.0%	0.0%	0.0%
Other**	$112,879	$117,563	$102,369	$99,025
	0.9%	0.8%	0.7%	0.8%
Total	$12,466,358	$15,145,998	$14,149,859	$13,110,958
	100.0%	100.0%	100.0%	100.0%

* Because of rounding, sums of percentages may not equal 100 percent.

** Expenditures for audio-visual are included in the "All Others" category to avoid potential disclosure of individual company data.

TABLE 2D

CIGARETTE ADVERTISING AND PROMOTIONAL EXPENDITURES FOR 2006-2010
(DOLLARS IN THOUSANDS)*

	2006	2007	2008	2009	2010
Newspapers	N/A	N/A	$169 0.0%	N/A	N/A
Magazines	$50,293 0.0%	$47,203 0.4%	$25,478 0.3%	$36,680 0.4%	$46,463 0.6%
Outdoor	$935 0.0%	$3,041 0.0%	$2,045 0.0%	$1,812 0.0%	$1,744 0.0%
Transit	$0 0.0%	$0 0.0%	$0 0.0%	$0 0.0%	$0 0.0%
Point-of-Sale	$242,625 1.9%	$198,861 1.9%	$163,709 1.0%	$110,311 1.3%	$106,634 1.3%
Price Discounts	$9,205,106 73.7%	$7,699,362 70.9%	$7,171,092 72.1%	$6,672,428 78.2%	$6,490,832 80.7%
Promotional Allowances – Retailers	$434,239 3.5%	$454,139 4.2%	$481,500 4.8%	$428,675 5.0%	$369,992 4.6%
Promotional Allowances – Wholesalers	$471,204 3.8%	$479,032 4.4%	$448,461 4.5%	$449,006 5.3%	$410,370 5.1%
Promotional Allowances – Other	N/A	N/A	$1,245 0.0%	$965 0.0%	$210 0.0%
Sampling Distribution	$29,431 0.2%	$48,719 0.4%	$54,261 0.5%	$23,784 0.3%	$22,166 0.3%
Specialty Item Distribution – Branded	$5,546 0.0%	$8,070 0.0%	$7,188 0.1%	$7,472 0.1%	$6,322 0.1%
Specialty Item Distribution – Non-Branded	$163,761 1.3%	$160,047 1.5%	$93,798 0.9%	$74,956 0.9%	$65,574 0.8%
Public Entertainment – Adult-Only	$168,098 1.3%	$160,104 1.5%	$154,749 1.5%	$134,328 1.6%	$138,889 1.7%
Public Entertainment – General-Audience	N/A	N/A	N/A	N/A	N/A
Sponsorships	N/A	N/A	N/A	N/A	$0 0.0%
Endorsements & Testimonials	$0 0.0%	$0 0.0%	$0 0.0%	$0 0.0%	$0 0.0%
Direct Mail	$102,353 0.8%	$81,929 0.8%	$89,920 0.9%	$68,891 0.8%	$56,482 0.7%
Coupons	$625,777 5.0%	$366,779 3.4%	$359,793 3.6%	$371,028 4.3%	$235,802 2.9%
Retail-Value-Added – Bonus Cigarettes	$817,792 6.5%	$981,566 9.0%	$721,818 7.3%	$11,736 0.1%	N/A **
Retail-Value-Added – Non-Cigarette Bonus	$14,642 0.1%	$17,720 0.1%	$10,983 0.1%	N/A	$0 0.0%
Company Website	$6,497 0.1%	$2,351 0.0%	$13,172 0.1%	$18,300 0.2%	$20,829 0.3%
Internet – Other	$0 0.0%	N/A	N/A	N/A	N/A
Telephone	N/A	N/A	N/A	N/A	N/A
Audio-Visual	$0 0.0%	$0 0.0%	$0 0.0%	$0 0.0%	$0 0.0%
Social Media				$0 0.0%	$0 0.0%
All Others**	$151,392 1.2%	$155,843 1.4%	$143,688 1.4%	$122,002 1.4%	$73,291 0.9%
Total	$12,489,692	$10,864,767	$9,943,068	$8,531,375	$8,045,602

* Because of rounding, sums of percentages may not equal 100 percent.
** Expenditures denoted "N/A" are included in the "All Others" category to avoid potential disclosure of individual company data.

TABLE 2E

CIGARETTE ADVERTISING AND PROMOTIONAL EXPENDITURES FOR 2011-2013
(DOLLARS IN THOUSANDS)*

	2011	2012	2013
Newspapers	$549 0.0%	N/A	N/A
Magazines	$23,254 0.3%	$27,943 0.3%	$50,609 0.6%
Outdoor	$3,100 0.0%	$2,211 0.0%	$2,269 0.0%
Transit	$0 0.0%	$0 0.0%	$0 0.0%
Point-of-Sale	$76,613 0.9%	$67,877 0.7%	$55,684 0.6%
Price Discounts	$6,996,942 83.6%	$7,802,044 85.1%	$7,642,441 85.4%
Promotional Allowances – Retailers	$356,991 4.3%	$335,129 3.7%	$291,334 3.3%
Promotional Allowances – Wholesalers	$401,006 4.8%	$391,146 4.3%	$397,182 4.4%
Promotional Allowances – Other	N/A	N/A	$548 0.0%
Sampling Distribution	$4,515 0.0%	N/A	N/A
Specialty Item Distribution – Branded	$5,607 0.0%	$1,683 0.0%	$2,974 0.0%
Specialty Item Distribution - Non-Branded	$44,394 0.5%	$26,116 0.3%	$29,504 0.3%
Public Entertainment – Adult-Only	$129,822 1.6%	$113,581 1.2%	$104,647 1.2%
Public Entertainment – General-Audience	$0 0.0%	N/A	$0 0.0%
Sponsorships	$0 0.0%	$0 0.0%	$0 0.0%
Endorsements & Testimonials	$0 0.0%	N/A	$0 0.0%
Direct Mail	$51,491 0.6%	$45,582 0.5%	$38,294 0.4%
Coupons	$171,222 2.0%	$239,618 2.6%	$248,833 2.8%
Retail-Value-Added – Bonus Cigarettes	$0 0.0%	$0 0.0%	$0 0.0%
Retail-Value-Added – Non-Cigarette Bonus	$0 0.0%	$0 0.0%	$0 0.0%
Company Website	$21,898 0.3%	$21,403 0.2%	$15,402 0.2%
Internet – Other	N/A	$1,309 0.0%	N/A
Telephone	N/A	N/A	N/A
Audio-Visual	$0 0.0%	N/A	$0 0.0%
Social Media	$0 0.0%	$0 0.0%	$0 0.0%
All Others**	$78,220 0.9%	$93,182 1.0%	$68,489 0.8%
Total	$8,365,624	$9,167,824	$8,948,210

* Because of rounding, sums of percentages may not equal 100 percent.

** Expenditures denoted "N/A" are included in the "All Others" category to avoid potential disclosure of individual company data.

TABLE 3

DOMESTIC CIGARETTE ADVERTISING EXPENDITURES
BY MEDIA FOR YEARS 1963 - 1974*
(MILLIONS OF DOLLARS)

YEAR	TV	RADIO	NEWSPAPER	MAGAZINES	DIRECT	BILLBOARD/ POSTER/ OUTDOOR/ TRANSIT	OTHER	TOTAL
1963	151.7	31.6	45.6		13.2		7.4	249.5
1964	170.2	25.5	45.2		14.6		5.8	261.3
1965	175.6	24.8	41.9		14.7		6.0	263.0
1966	198.0	31.3	43.4		17.9		6.9	297.5
1967	226.9	17.5	41.2		20.3		6.0	311.5
1968	217.2	21.3	44.6		21.6		6.0	310.7
1969	221.3	13.6	48.7		13.4		8.9	305.9
1970	205.0	12.4	14.7	49.5	16.9	11.7	4.5	314.7
1971	2.2	0	59.3	98.3	27.0	60.6	4.2	251.6
1972	0	0	63.1	96.1	22.9	67.5	8.0	257.6
1973	0	0	65.3	92.4	15.2	63.2	11.4	247.5
1974	0	0	80.5	114.6	31.1	71.4	9.2	306.8

*   The data reported in Tables 2 through 2E were not collected in their present form until 1975. Thus, Table 3, which reports cigarette advertising expenditures from 1963 through 1974, has been retained in this report for comparative purposes.

Year	Market share of cigarettes having tar yields of:				
	15 mg. or less	12 mg. or less	9 mg. or less	6 mg. or less	3 mg. or less
1967	2.0%				
1968	2.5%				
1969	3.0%				
1970	3.6%				
1971	3.8%				
1972	6.6%				
1973	8.9%				
1974	8.9%				
1975	13.5%				
1976	15.9%				
1977	22.7%				
1978	27.5%				
1979	40.9%				
1980	44.8%				
1981	56.0%				
1982	52.2%	43.8%	27.8%	8.9%	2.9%
1983	53.1%	44.9%	27.9%	9.4%	3.1%
1984	51.0%	43.4%	26.3%	9.4%	2.9%
1985	51.9%	43.1%	25.3%	8.4%	2.3%
1986	52.6%	44.5%	22.3%	9.9%	2.6%
1987	55.4%	47.8%	20.2%	10.0%	2.5%
1988	54.2%	48.7%	20.1%	10.7%	3.1%
1989	55.1%	48.4%	21.5%	11.4%	2.4%
1990	60.6%	51.5%	25.5%	12.2%	2.8%

TABLE 4
DOMESTIC MARKET SHARE OF CIGARETTES BY TAR YIELD

TABLE 4A DOMESTIC MARKET SHARE OF CIGARETTES BY TAR YIELD					
Year	Market share of cigarettes having tar yields of:				
	15 mg. or less	12 mg. or less	9 mg. or less	6 mg. or less	3 mg. or less
1991	60.5%	52.6%	22.0%	12.7%	2.6%
1992	68.7%	52.9%	24.9%	12.7%	2.5%
1993	66.5%	53.3%	23.4%	12.6%	1.9%
1994	71.2%	53.7%	23.1%	12.3%	2.1%
1995	72.7%	53.6%	27.1%	12.2%	2.2%
1996	67.4%	55.5%	22.3%	11.9%	1.9%
1997	70.2%	55.6%	21.9%	11.5%	1.7%
1998	81.9%	56.8%	22.9%	13.2%	1.6%
1999	86.6%	57.4%	25.3%	13.6%	1.6%
2000	87.1%	50.4%	23.7%	13.6%	1.3%
2001	85.2%	58.1%	22.6%	13.2%	1.0%
2002	84.9%	58.2%	22.5%	12.9%	0.9%
2003	84.9%	59.5%	22.5%	12.6%	0.8%
2004	84.8%	57.7%	19.2%	11.5%	0.8%
2005	83.5%	58.4%	18.7%	11.5%	0.6%
2006	84.4%	57.7%	19.5%	11.1%	0.5%
2007	82.7%	57.3%	19.6%	10.7%	0.4%
2008	84.3%	57.6%	18.0%	10.3%	0.3%
2009	74.7%	54.4%	15.5%	9.6%	0.3%
2010	86.4%	53.8%	12.9%	8.3%	0.2%
2011*	94.2%	53.4%	12.2%	8.0%	0.2%
2012*	88.8%	54.8%	20.7%	13.0%	5.0%
2013*	87.3%	52.7%	14.0%	7.4%	0.3%

* Prior to 2011, the companies were required to submit tar, nicotine, and carbon monoxide yield data for every cigarette variety they sold. Since 2011, the companies have only been required to submit data in their possession or control; the Commission has not required them to test their cigarettes. As a result, market share comparisons both within a given year and to previous years might no longer be accurate.

TABLE 5

DOMESTIC MARKET SHARE OF FILTER AND NON-FILTER CIGARETTES
(1963-1986)

YEAR	NON-FILTER	FILTER	CHARCOAL	NON-CHARCOAL
1963	42%	58%	*	*
1964	39%	61%	*	*
1965	36%	64%	*	*
1966	32%	68%	*	*
1967	28%	72%	*	*
1968	26%	74%	6%	68%
1969	23%	77%	6%	71%
1970	20%	80%	6%	74%
1971	18%	82%	6%	76%
1972	16%	84%	6%	77%
1973	15%	85%	5%	80%
1974	14%	86%	5%	81%
1975	13%	87%	5%	82%
1976	12%	88%	4%	84%
1977	10%	90%	4%	86%
1978	10%	90%	3%	87%
1979	9%	91%	3%	88%
1980	8%	92%	3%	89%
1981	8%	92%	2%	90%
1982	7%	93%	2%	91%
1983	7%	93%	2%	91%
1984	7%	93%	2%	91%
1985	6%	94%	1%	93%
1986	6%	94%	1%	93%

*   Figures for charcoal filter cigarettes for the years 1963 through 1967 were not obtained.

TABLE 5A

DOMESTIC MARKET SHARE OF FILTER AND NON-FILTER CIGARETTES
(1987-2013)

YEAR	NON-FILTER	FILTER
1987	4%	96%
1988	5%	95%
1989	5%	95%
1990	5%	95%
1991	4%	96%
1992	3%	97%
1993	3%	97%
1994	3%	97%
1995	3%	97%
1996	3%	97%
1997	2%	98%
1998	2%	98%
1999	2%	98%
2000	2%	98%
2001	2%	98%
2002	2%	98%
2003	1%	99%
2004	1%	99%
2005	1%	99%
2006	1%	99%
2007	1%	99%
2008	1%	99%
2009	0.5%	99.5%
2010	0.5%	99.5%
2011	0.4%	99.6%
2012	0.3%	99.7%
2013	0.3%	99.7%

TABLE 6

DOMESTIC MARKET SHARE OF CIGARETTES BY LENGTH IN MILLIMETERS

YEAR	68-72 mm	79-88 mm (King)	94-101 mm (Long)	110-121 mm
1967	14%	77%	9%	---
1968	12%	74%	13%	---
1969	11%	74%	16%	---
1970	9%	73%	18%	---
1971	8%	72%	20%	---
1972	8%	71%	21%	---
1973	7%	71%	22%	---
1974	6%	71%	23%	--- *
1975	6%	69%	24%	1%
1976	5%	69%	24%	2%
1977	5%	67%	26%	2%
1978	5%	65%	27%	2%
1979	4%	65%	30%	2%
1980	3%	63%	32%	2%
1981	3%	62%	33%	2%
1982	3%	61%	34%	2%
1983	3%	60%	34%	2%
1984	3%	59%	36%	2%
1985	3%	58%	37%	2%
1986	2%	58%	37%	3%
1987	2%	57%	38%	3%
1988	2%	57%	38%	2%
1989	2%	57%	39%	2%
1990	2%	57%	39%	2%
1991	2%	56%	40%	2%
1992	2%	56%	41%	2%
1993	1%	55%	42%	2%
1994	1%	56%	41%	2%
1995	1%	57%	40%	2%
1996	1%	57%	40%	2%
1997	1%	58%	39%	2%
1998	1%	59%	38%	2%
1999	1%	59%	38%	2%
2000	1%	60%	37%	2%
2001	1%	60%	38%	1%
2002	1%	61%	37%	2%
2003	1%	61%	36%	2%
2004	1%	62%	35%	2%
2005	1%	62%	35%	2%
2006	1%	62%	35%	2%
2007	1%	65%	32%	2%
2008	2%	61%	34%	2%
2009	2%	61%	35%	2%
2010	3%	59%	36%	2%
2011	3%	57%	38%	2%
2012	3%	56%	39%	1%
2013**	3%	57%	39%	1%

* The 110-121 mm length was combined with 94-101 mm length.
** The table does not report the less than 0.1% share of cigarettes with a 93 mm length.

TABLE 7

DOMESTIC MARKET SHARE OF MENTHOL AND NON-MENTHOL CIGARETTES
(1963-2000)

YEAR	MENTHOL	NON-MENTHOL
1963	16%	84%
1964	16%	84%
1965	18%	82%
1966	19%	81%
1967	20%	80%
1968	21%	79%
1969	22%	78%
1970	23%	77%
1971	24%	76%
1972	24%	76%
1973	25%	75%
1974	27%	73%
1975	27%	73%
1976	28%	72%
1977	28%	72%
1978	28%	72%
1979	29%	71%
1980	28%	72%
1981	28%	72%
1982	29%	71%
1983	28%	72%
1984	28%	72%
1985	28%	72%
1986	28%	72%
1987	28%	72%
1988	28%	72%
1989	27%	73%
1990	26%	74%
1991	27%	73%
1992	26%	74%
1993	26%	74%
1994	25%	75%
1995	25%	75%
1996	25%	75%
1997	25%	75%
1998	26%	74%
1999	26%	74%
2000	26%	74%

TABLE 7A

DOMESTIC MARKET SHARE OF MENTHOL AND NON-MENTHOL CIGARETTES
(2001 – 2013)

YEAR	MENTHOL	NON-MENTHOL
2001	26%	74%
2002	27%	73%
2003	27%	73%
2004	27%	73%
2005	27%	73%
2006	28%	72%
2007	29%	71%
2008	27%	73%
2009	29%	71%
2010	31%	69%
2011	32%	68%
2012	31%	69%
2013	31%	69%

TABLE 8

DISCLOSURE OF TAR AND NICOTINE RATINGS ON CIGARETTE PACKS (1994 - 2001)

		1994	1995	1996	1997	1998	1999	2000	2001
% of overall market that discloses ratings on the pack		6.3%	6.3%	6.1%	5.8%	5.3%	4.1%	3.6%	1.8%
more than 15 mg. tar	market share of varieties in tar group	28.8%	27.3%	32.7%	29.8%	18.0%	13.4%	12.9%	14.8%
	% that discloses ratings on pack	0.0%	0.0%	0.0%	0.0%	0.0%	0.0%	0.0%	0.0%
12-15 mg. tar	market share of varieties in tar group	19.3%	21.0%	15.3%	16.7%	29.1%	32.5%	39.0%	29.7%
	% that discloses ratings on pack	0.0%	0.1%	0.1%	0.1%	0.1%	0.1%	0.1%	0.0%
8-11 mg. tar	market share of varieties in tar group	38.6%	38.7%	39.2%	41.0%	39.4%	40.3%	33.9%	42.1%
	% that discloses ratings on pack	2.4%	2.8%	2.6%	2.3%	3.2%	1.6%	0.7%	1.0%
4-7 mg. tar	market share of varieties in tar group	11.2%	10.8%	10.9%	10.8%	11.9%	12.2%	12.9%	12.5%
	% that discloses ratings on pack	30.7%	30.1%	29.3%	28.6%	20.7%	16.2%	16.5%	3.7%
3 mg. tar or less	market share of varieties in tar group	2.1%	2.2%	1.9%	1.7%	1.6%	1.6%	1.3%	1.0%
	% that discloses ratings on pack	91.8%	89.1%	97.2%	97.3%	97.4%	92.3%	92.0%	87.9%

TABLE 8A
DISCLOSURE OF TAR RATINGS ON CIGARETTE PACKS (2002-2011)*

		2002	2003	2004	2005	2006	2007	2008	2009	2010	2011
% of overall market that discloses ratings on the pack		1.4%	1.2%	1.2%	0.9%	0.8%	0.8%	0.0%	0.0%	0.0%	0.0%
more than 15 mg. tar	market share of varieties in group	15.1%	15.1%	15.2%	16.5%	15.5%	17.3%	15.7%	25.2%	13.6%	5.8%
	% that discloses ratings on pack	0.0%	0.0%	0.0%	0.0%	0.0%	0.0%	0.0%	0.0%	0.0%	0.0%
12-15 mg. tar	market share of varieties in group	28.8%	28.9%	30.3%	28.3%	28.4%	27.4%	29.9%	23.1%	33.5%	46.5.%
	% that discloses ratings on pack	0.0%	0.0%	0.0%	0.0%	0.0%	0.0%	0.0%	0.0%	0.0%	0.0%
8-11 mg. tar	market share of varieties in group	43.0%	43.2%	42.5%	43.3%	44.5%	44.3%	43.7%	41.8%	43.9%	38.8%
	% that discloses ratings on pack	0.9%	0.8%	0.7%	0.6%	0.5%	0.5%	0.0%	0.0%	0.0%	0.0%
4-7 mg. tar	market share of varieties in group	12.2%	12.0%	11.2%	11.3%	10.9%	10.5%	10.3%	9.7%	8.7%	8.6.%
	% that discloses ratings on pack	1.8%	1.5%	1.5%	1.2%	1.0%	0.8%	0.0%	0.0%	0.0%	0.0%
3 mg. tar or less	market share of varieties in group	0.9%	0.8%	0.8%	0.6%	0.5%	0.4%	0.3%	0.3%	0.2%	0.2%
	% that discloses ratings on pack	88.7%	89.9%	91.6%	90.7%	94.9%	100.0%	0.0%	0.0%	0.0%	0.0%

* Prior to 2011, the companies were required to submit tar yield data for every cigarette variety they sold. Since 2011, the companies have only been required to submit data in their possession or control; the Commission has not required them to test every one of their cigarettes. As a result, market share comparisons both within a given year and to previous years might no longer be accurate. Given that and the fact that since 2008 the companies have reported that they have not disclosed tar ratings on any of their packs, the Commission will no longer be updating this table.

APPENDIX

2013 Advertising and Promotional Expenditure Categories

Newspapers: Newspaper advertising; but excluding expenditures in connection with sampling, specialty item distribution, public entertainment, endorsements, sponsorships, coupons, and retail-value-added.

Magazines: Magazine advertising; but excluding expenditures in connection with sampling, specialty item distribution, public entertainment, endorsements, sponsorships, coupons, and retail-value-added.

Outdoor: Billboards; signs and placards in arenas, stadiums, and shopping malls, whether they are open air or enclosed; and any other advertisements placed outdoors, regardless of their size, including those on cigarette retailer property; but excluding expenditures in connection with sampling, specialty item distribution, public entertainment, endorsements, sponsorships, coupons, and retail-value-added.

Audio-visual: Audio-visual or video advertising on any medium of electronic communication not subject to the Federal Communications Commission's jurisdiction, including screens at motion picture theaters, video cassettes or DVDs, and television screens or monitors in stores; but excluding expenditures in connection with Internet advertising.

Transit: Advertising on or within private or public vehicles and all advertisements placed at, on or within any bus stop, taxi stand, transportation waiting area, train station, airport, or any other transportation facility; but excluding expenditures in connection with sampling, specialty item distribution, public entertainment, endorsements, sponsorships, coupons, and retail-value-added.

Point-of-Sale: Point-of-sale advertisements; but excluding expenditures in connection with outdoor advertising, sampling, specialty item distribution, public entertainment, endorsements, sponsorships, coupons, and retail-value-added.

Price discounts: Price discounts paid to cigarette retailers or wholesalers in order to reduce the price of cigarettes to consumers, including off-invoice discounts, buy-downs, voluntary price reductions, and trade programs; but excluding retail-value-added expenditures for promotions involving free cigarettes and expenditures involving coupons.

Promotional Allowances – Retail: Promotional allowances paid to cigarette retailers in order to facilitate the sale or placement of any cigarette, including payments for stocking, shelving, displaying and merchandising brands, volume rebates, incentive payments, and the cost of cigarettes given to retailers for free for subsequent sale to consumers; but excluding expenditures in connection with newspapers, magazines, outdoor, audio-visual, transit, direct mail, point-of-sale, and price discounts.

Promotional Allowances – Wholesale: Promotional allowances paid to cigarette wholesalers in order to facilitate the sale or placement of any cigarette, including payments for volume rebates, incentive payments, value added services, promotional execution and satisfaction of reporting requirements; but excluding expenditures in connection with newspapers, magazines, outdoor, audio-visual, transit, direct mail, point-of-sale, price discounts, and retail promotional allowances.

Promotional Allowances – Other: Promotional allowances paid to any persons other than retailers, wholesalers, and full-time company employees who are involved in the cigarette distribution and sales process in order to facilitate the sale or placement of any cigarette; but excluding expenditures in connection with newspapers, magazines, outdoor, audio-visual, transit, direct mail, point-of-sale, price discounts, and retail and wholesale promotional allowances.

Sampling: Sampling of cigarettes, including the cost of the cigarettes, all associated excise taxes and increased costs under the Master Settlement Agreement, and the cost of organizing, promoting, and conducting sampling. Sampling includes the distribution of cigarettes for consumer testing or evaluation when consumers are able to smoke the cigarettes outside of a facility operated by the Company, but not the cost of actual clinical testing or market research associated with such cigarette distributions. Sampling also includes the distribution of coupons for free cigarettes, when no purchase or payment is required to obtain the coupons or cigarettes.

Specialty Item Distribution – Branded: All costs of distributing any item (other than cigarettes, items the sole function of which is to advertise or promote cigarettes, or written or electronic publications), whether distributed by sale, redemption of coupons, or otherwise, that bears the name, logo, or an image of any portion of the package of any brand or variety of cigarettes, including the cost of the items distributed but subtracting any payments received for the item. The costs associated with distributing non-cigarette items in connection with sampling or retail-value-added programs are reported in those categories, not as specialty item distribution.

Specialty Item Distribution – Non-Branded: All costs of distributing any item (other than cigarettes, items the sole function of which is to advertise or promote cigarettes, or written or electronic publications), whether distributed by sale, redemption of coupons, or otherwise, that does not bear the name, logo, or an image of any portion of the package of any brand or variety of cigarette, including the cost of the items distributed but subtracting any payments received for the item. The costs associated with distributing non-cigarette items in connection with sampling or retail-value-added programs are reported in those categories, not as specialty item distribution.

Direct Mail: Direct mail advertising; but excluding expenditures in connection with sampling, specialty item distribution, public entertainment, endorsements, sponsorships, coupons, retail-value-added, and Internet advertising.

Public Entertainment – Adult-Only: Public entertainment events bearing or otherwise displaying the name or logo or an image of any portion of the package of any of a company's cigarettes or otherwise referring or relating to cigarettes, which take place in an adult-only facility, including all expenditures made by the company in promoting and/or sponsoring such events.

Public Entertainment – General-Audience: Public entertainment events bearing or otherwise displaying the name or logo or an image of any portion of the package of any of a company's cigarettes or otherwise referring or relating to cigarettes, which do not take place in an adult-only facility, including all expenditures made by the company in promoting and/or sponsoring such events.

Retail-Value-Added – Bonus Cigarettes: Retail-value-added expenditures for promotions involving free cigarettes (*e.g.,* buy two packs, get one free), whether or not the free cigarettes are physically bundled together with the purchased cigarettes, including all expenditures and costs associated with the value added to the purchase of cigarettes (*e.g.,* excise taxes paid for the free cigarettes and increased costs under the Master Settlement Agreement).

Retail-Value-Added – Non-Cigarette Bonus: Retail-value-added expenditures for promotions involving free non-cigarettes items (*e.g.,* buy two packs, get a cigarette lighter), including all expenditures and costs associated with the value added to the purchase of cigarettes.

Coupons: All costs associated with coupons for the reduction of the retail cost of cigarettes, whether redeemed at the point-of-sale or by mail, including all costs associated with advertising or promotion, design, printing, distribution, and redemption. However, when coupons are distributed for free cigarettes and no purchase or payment is required to obtain the coupons or the cigarettes, these activities are considered to be sampling and not couponing.

Sponsorships: Sponsorships of sports teams or individual athletes, but excluding endorsements.

Endorsements & Testimonials: Endorsements, testimonials, and product placement.

Company Website: All expenditures associated with advertising on any company Internet website.

Internet – Other: Internet advertising other than on the Company's own Internet website, including on the World Wide Web, on commercial on-line services, and through electronic mail messages; but excluding costs associated with social media marketing.

Telephone: Telephone advertising, including costs associated with the placement of telemarketing calls or the operation of incoming telephone lines that allow consumers to participate in any promotion or hear pre-recorded product messages; but excluding costs associated with having customer service representatives available for responding to consumer complaints or questions.

Social Media Marketing: All expenditures for social media marketing on Web sites or other online services or communities, including but not limited to social networking sites, microblogging sites, content-sharing sites, and blogs.

All Other: Advertising and promotional expenditures not covered by another category.